ECO-ACTION

Consumerism
of the Future

Angela Royston

Heinemann
LIBRARY

H www.heinemann.co.uk/library

Visit our website to find out more information about **Heinemann Library** books.

To order:

☎ Phone 44 (0) 1865 888066

▤ Send a fax to 44 (0) 1865 314091

▣ Visit the Heinemann Bookshop at **www.heinemann.co.uk/library** to browse our catalogue and order online.

First published in Great Britain by Heinemann Library, Halley Court, Jordan Hill, Oxford OX2 8EJ, part of Harcourt Education.
Heinemann is a registered trademark of Harcourt Education Ltd.

© Harcourt Education Ltd 2008
The moral right of the proprietor has been asserted.

Editorial: Catherine Veitch and Melanie Waldron
Design: Philippa Jenkins and Michelle Lisseter
Illustrations: Bridge Creative Services p.8;
    Jeff Edwards p.17; Philippa Jenkins pp.12, 13
Picture Research: Melissa Allison
Production: Alison Parsons

Originated by Chroma Graphics (Overseas) Pte. Ltd
Printed and bound in China by South China Printing Co. Ltd.

ISBN 978 0 4310 2988 7
12 11 10 09 08
10 9 8 7 6 5 4 3 2 1

British Library Cataloguing in Publication Data
Royston, Angela
Consumerism of the future. - (Eco-action)
339.4'7

A full catalogue record for this book is available from the British Library.

Acknowledgements
The publishers would like to thank the following for permission to reproduce photographs:
©Alamy pp. **35** (blickwinkel/Huetter), **14** (Brian North), **23** (G P Bowater), **29** (mediacolor's), **43** (Melvyn Longhurst), **22** (Worldwide Picture Library/Sue Cunningham); ©Corbis pp. **27** (Bill Stormont), **7** (Gideon Mendel), **32** (Louie Psihoyos), **20** (Macduff Everton); ©Dreamstime.com pp. **21** (Alexander Ivanov), **18** (Elena Elisseeva), **4** (Heng Kong Chen), **19** (Lockstockbob), **28** (Peter Pomorski), **37** (Yana Petruseva); ©FLPA pp. **25** (Inga Spence), **24** (Nigel Cattlin); ©Getty Images pp. **6** (AFP/STR), **5** (Stone/Jaime Villaseca), **38** (Stone/Philip & Karen Smith); ©Harcourt Education Ltd pp. **11**, **30**, **33** (Tudor Photography); ©istockphoto.com pp. **41** (Arthur Kwiatkowsk), **42** (Todd Smith); ©NHPA p. **9** (Bill Coster); ©Photolibrary p. **17** (Maximilian Stock Ltd); ©Still Pictures pp. **31** (argus/Peter Frischmuth), **39** (Jorgen Schytte), **26** (Nick Cobbing), **36** (Peter Hirth), **34** (Roger Braithwaite), **15** (Ron Giling), **10** (ullstein – Oed).

Cover photograph of fresh apples, variety Jazz, reproduced with permission of Photolibrary.

Every effort has been made to contact copyright holders of any material reproduced in this book. Any omissions will be rectified in subsequent printings if notice is given to the publishers.

Contents

Any words appearing in the text in bold, **like this**, are explained in the Glossary.

Shopping bonanza

Consumers in Europe, North America, Japan, and Australia are enjoying a shopping bonanza. Racks of cheap clothes, computers, DVD players, CD players, and televisions fill our stores. Many people change their mobile phones every year, and supermarket shelves are crammed with every kind of food all year round. The range of goods becomes wider and their prices ever cheaper.

Cheap and cheerful

The cheaper goods become, the more people in **developed countries** buy. The companies who manufacture the goods are often very large. They carry out their operations around the world and spend huge sums of money on advertising and marketing to persuade people that buying their goods will make them happy.

Who pays the price?

The majority of people in the countries where many of the goods are manufactured do not share this shopping bonanza. Most goods are made in China, India, Pakistan, and countries in South-East Asia and Latin America and then transported to other countries around the world. The goods are cheap because the workers in these countries are paid very low wages – so low that sometimes children have to work so their families can survive.

Shopping centres are crammed with cheap goods.

The Earth's resources

Electronic and many other goods are made mostly from metals and other materials found in the ground. Plastic and other **synthetic materials**, for example, are made from oil. These materials are all part of the Earth's resources. Some materials are plentiful, but others are in short supply.

Factories use machinery that runs on electricity to manufacture goods. The electricity is generated in power stations, usually by burning coal, oil, or natural gas. These are called **fossil fuels** and they are part of the Earth's resources too. So consumerism, that is the production and sale of more and more goods, is using up more and more of the Earth's resources. It is also causing an even bigger problem – **global warming**.

This mine in Zambia extracts copper that is sold to companies in the West.

EXPLOIT OR CONSERVE?
Many companies and governments act as though the Earth's resources are there for them to exploit as they like. Other people think the Earth's resources should be used carefully and preserved for future generations. Do you think how companies use resources and treat people in other countries should be more strictly **regulated**?

Hidden costs

The way that most companies and most farmers produce goods and food is wasting the Earth's resources and contributing to the greatest problem of all – global warming. The temperature of the Earth is becoming warmer and this is causing climates around the world to change more rapidly than ever before. Global warming and **climate change** threaten the world with catastrophes that could kill millions of people and make life very difficult for billions more.

In Navarra, northern Spain, the River Ebro burst its banks, flooding the highway.

Climate change

As the world gets warmer, **droughts** will become more common in many parts of the world. Deserts such as the Sahara, which is already spreading farther south into Africa, will spread even faster. Droughts cause people's food crops to fail and their cattle to die, creating famine and making people more likely to succumb to disease.

Climate change will bring more extreme weather. Heavy rain in some areas will cause rivers to rise, flooding large areas of farmland. Severe **hurricanes** and **typhoons** will become more common. The year 2005 was a particularly bad year for hurricanes, with many storms, including Hurricane Katrina, battering the islands of the Caribbean and the southern coast of the United States. Storms like these can kill people and cause millions of pounds worth of damage.

Long-term effects

The long-term effects of global warming are even more serious. As temperatures rise worldwide, thick ice in the Arctic and Antarctic will begin to melt. When land ice melts, extra water pours into the world's oceans, causing the sea level to rise. As sea levels rise, low-lying coastal areas will be flooded. If we do not act to reduce and stop global warming even cities such as New York and London will eventually be flooded.

Changes in climate have happened before, but they have occurred over thousands of years. People can adapt to climate change – if they have time. But today the Earth is warming so fast there is not enough time for most people and countries to prepare for it.

WHO SHOULD TAKE RESPONSIBILITY?
The people who will suffer the most from climate change are the world's poorest people. They are the ones for whom drought, disease, and flooding will be most severe and they are the ones who can least afford to cope with these catastrophes. Climate change is caused mainly by the way developed countries use the Earth's resources and burn fossil fuels. Should people in these countries take responsibility for their actions? If so, we must change the way we live to avoid the worst effects of climate change.

In 2006 a severe drought in East Africa killed thousands of cattle, destroying the main source of local people's food.

Living in a greenhouse

How does mining the Earth's resources and burning fossil fuels cause global warming? The answer lies in the gas **carbon dioxide** and certain other gases that are produced when fossil fuels are burned. They are also produced during some industrial processes. Carbon dioxide occurs naturally in the atmosphere. It is produced by living things as they breathe out and when they die. The bodies of living things are composed largely of carbon and, as they decompose or are burned, the carbon combines with oxygen in the air to make more carbon dioxide. This carbon dioxide is not the cause of the problem, however, because it is recycled by plants to make food, in a process called **photosynthesis**. Global warming is caused by the billions of tonnes of additional carbon dioxide produced every year by burning fossil fuels.

The greenhouse effect

Carbon dioxide causes global warming because, like a greenhouse, it traps the Sun's heat. As the Sun's heat shines down, most of it is absorbed by the land and the sea while the rest is reflected back into the atmosphere. The absorbed heat is then released and, provided much of it escapes back into space, the temperature stays fairly even, making it possible for life to exist. Excess carbon dioxide in the air, however, is now trapping this released heat, making the Earth warmer.

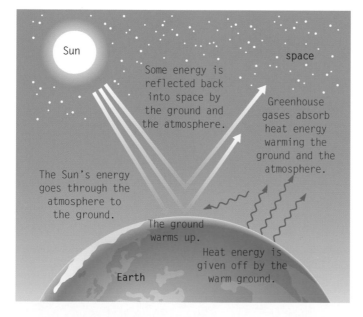

Sun

space

Some energy is reflected back into space by the ground and the atmosphere.

Greenhouse gases absorb heat energy warming the ground and the atmosphere.

The Sun's energy goes through the atmosphere to the ground.

The ground warms up.

Heat energy is given off by the warm ground.

Earth

Carbon dioxide in the air stops heat escaping. This warms the air below, acting like a greenhouse.

Actual greenhouses are useful. Plants grow in the warmer air that would not grow so well in the colder air outside.

Why is global warming happening now?

For thousands of years people produced very little extra carbon dioxide. They fertilized farm crops with animal manure and they made many goods from wood. The population of the world was lower and most people owned fewer clothes and other goods. They did not have electricity, motor vehicles, or aeroplanes, and they had not discovered how to turn oil into plastic and other synthetic materials. These discoveries have all come in the last 100 years and have transformed the way we live. But they have also led to the burning of billions of tonnes of fossil fuels and the addition of about 35 billion tonnes (about 40 billion tons) of extra carbon dioxide to the atmosphere each year.

Most power stations burn coal, oil, or gas to generate electricity. Factories, warehouses, and shops that make and sell consumer goods all use large amounts of electricity.

Fossil fuels

Fossil fuels formed millions of years ago from the remains of plants and animals. Coal formed from the remains of huge forests that grew about 300 million years ago, before the dinosaurs roamed the Earth. Oil and natural gas formed from the remains of tiny marine organisms that lived even earlier.

Mining and drilling

People mine for coal. Machines cut coal from rocks and it is taken, often in trains, to **power stations**. Here it is burned, heating water to create steam. The steam turns **turbines** and this generates electricity. Sometimes power stations buy coal from other countries, so the coal is transported hundreds or thousands of miles in ships and overland by road or rail.

Oil usually forms deep underground between layers of rocks. People drill through the rock to reach the oil and bring it to the surface. Some oil is pumped through pipes to an oil **refinery,** but much is carried by huge oil tankers that may sail half-way around the world.

OTHER GREENHOUSE GASES

Carbon dioxide is not the only **greenhouse gas**. Water vapour, **methane, nitrous oxide**, ozone, and **chlorofluorocarbons** (CFCs) are greenhouse gases too. After water vapour, carbon dioxide is the most abundant. The oceans, tropical **rainforests**, and other carbon "sinks" can absorb about half of the carbon dioxide we produce at present, but the rest creates the greenhouse effect.

Refining oil

Once oil reaches a refinery it is heated and separated into many different substances. Much of it is made into fuel for transport – petrol for road vehicles, diesel fuel for lorries, ships, and diesel trains, and kerosene for aircraft. Some of it is burned in power stations to generate electricity. The heaviest material is bitumen, a black tarry substance that is used on roads and roofs. The part of the oil that is made into petrol is also made into plastics and different chemicals, such as those used in fertilizers. Polythene and acrylics are used to make cloth, paints, glues, toys, packaging, and many other things. The list of things that are made from oil is almost endless and include some that might surprise you, such as medicines.

TOO VALUABLE TO BURN?

Because oil is the basis of so many materials that we now rely on, many people think that it is too precious to waste as fuel for transport and for power stations. There are still large supplies of oil under the ground, but even if we burned a quarter of them, the Earth would be subjected to irreversible, runaway global warming.

Some of the many products made from oil.

How shopping contributes to global warming

Most consumer goods contribute to global warming at every stage of their production and distribution. Machines use energy to extract raw materials, and vehicles burn fossil fuel to transport them to factories. Factories use energy to manufacture and package the goods, and ships and trucks burn diesel fuel to take the finished goods to warehouses and shops. Finally, shoppers often drive to and from stores and shopping malls, burning petrol in their cars.

From raw materials to finished goods

Most goods are made from materials that come from different parts of the world and the finished goods are often sold worldwide. For example, the trees that were pulped to make the paper for this book grew in North America or in Scandinavia. The paper was then shipped to China where it was printed and bound into books. The ink and glue were manufactured from oil and transported to the printer separately.

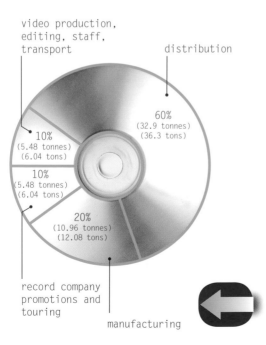

video production, editing, staff, transport

distribution

60%
(32.9 tonnes)
(36.3 tons)

10%
(5.48 tonnes)
(6.04 tons)

10%
(5.48 tonnes)
(6.04 tons)

20%
(10.96 tonnes)
(12.08 tons)

record company promotions and touring

manufacturing

MAKING AND DISTRIBUTING A SINGLE CD
One Swedish musician, Eric Prydz, discovered that producing and distributing 40,000 CDs of his single "Proper Education" created 54.8 tonnes (60.4 tons) of carbon dioxide. The diagram left shows how much of this came from manufacturing the CD, promoting it, and distributing it. More than half the carbon dioxide was produced by the lorries that transported the CD to shops across the country.

How different stages of the production and distribution of a CD single contribute to a total of 54.8 tonnes (60.4 tons) of carbon dioxide.

The finished books were shipped to Europe, North America, and countries around the world. In fact the book you are holding has probably travelled farther than most of its readers!

Unsustainable lifestyles

People in industrialized countries consume much more of the Earth's resources per person than the rest of the world. It has been calculated that, if everyone in the world shared the same lifestyle as the average person in the United States, it would take over five planets like Earth to supply the resources needed. Similarly, it would take more than three planets to provide everyone in the world with the same lifestyle as people in Britain enjoy. This is why people say that the way of life in developed countries is not sustainable. The following chapters look at different ways consumerism contributes to global warming and some of things we can do about it.

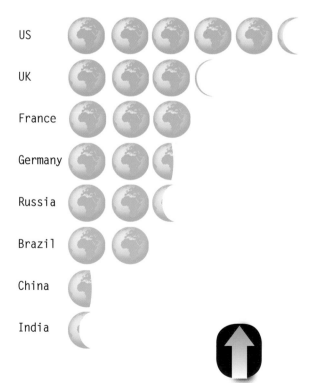

This diagram shows how many planet Earths it would take to provide the resources for everyone in the world to live like citizens of each of these countries.

CUTTING THE LINK

In the past most goods were made locally, so people knew how the goods were made and often the person who made them. Today most consumers have no idea how or where the things they buy were made. Some people think that cutting the link between the producer and the consumer makes people value goods less. What do you think?

Freight miles

Very few of the consumer goods that shoppers buy in Europe, North America, or Australia are actually manufactured in any of these countries. The companies that design and sell them pay factories in countries such as China and Korea to make them, because wages there are lower. This means that raw materials and consumer goods are being shipped back and forth across the world, and every journey involves vehicles of some kind burning fossil fuels. Farm produce is also transported around the world, and this can create additional problems.

Cotton

Cotton is one of the biggest crops grown in the south-east United States, but very little cotton is made into clothes in the US. Instead cotton that is grown in South Carolina may be shipped to Sudan in Africa to be spun and woven into cloth. Then the cloth is sent to a factory in Pakistan to be made into garments. The garments are then shipped back to the United States and to other countries.

Flowers from abroad

How is it that you can buy roses and other flowers all year round in supermarkets? The answer is that they are flown in from hot countries, such as Kenya and Ecuador. The flowers are **air-freighted** so they do not wilt and die before they reach the customer.

Aircraft produce much more carbon dioxide than ships.

These flowers are being grown in Brazil, South America, to be air-freighted to the United States and Europe, where they will be sold.

Air freighting is expensive, but the companies still make money because they pay the workers who grow and pick the flowers such low wages. And, by growing them in a country with a tropical climate, they can be grown and sold all year round.

Land and water

Importing flowers, fruit, and vegetables from abroad creates other problems. The flowers take up land that could be used to grow food for local people, and they can deprive local people of much needed water. In parts of Kenya, farmers claim that they can no longer support their families, because the companies that grow flowers are taking too much water from the River Ngiro, Kenya's second largest river.

Some companies in western countries have set up factories in **developing countries** to make soft drinks to sell in North America and Europe. The factories use so much water from underground supplies that the traditional wells have dried up. Similarly Israeli and Egyptian farmers grow fruit and vegetables to sell in Europe, although both countries have limited supplies of water. The Israelis take large amounts of water from underground supplies that they share with neighbouring countries and from the River Jordan, depriving local people of the water they need to grow food for themselves.

15

Food miles

Processed food contributes to global warming at almost every stage of its production, but particularly in transport and distribution, which accounts for about half the total carbon dioxide produced by the food industry. Most processed food is made and packed in factories. The ingredients for ready-made meals, biscuits, puddings, and other foods come from different places, often from different countries. Once the food is prepared, it is packed and transported to food depots, shops, and supermarkets. Customers often drive to and from shops and supermarkets.

The most extravagant form of transport is air-freighting. Tonnes of fruit and vegetables are flown around the world, producing more tonnes of carbon dioxide than the weight of the food itself. For example, pineapples air-freighted from Hawaii to the United States mainland produce ten times their own weight of carbon dioxide.

INTERNATIONAL INGREDIENTS

A box of chocolates is one example of a product that uses ingredients that are shipped from many different countries. The countries given here are just a few of the possible sources.

- Chocolate, made from cocoa beans from West Africa or Central America
- Sugar from the Caribbean
- Almonds from Spain
- Coffee (in coffee cream) from Brazil
- Hazelnuts from Turkey
- Oranges (in orange cup) from Spain or the United States
- Vanilla from Tahiti

Tropical fruit is delicious but is it worth damaging the planet to air-freight it to cooler countries?

Exotic fruit and vegetables

There are two main reasons why fruit and vegetables are air-freighted to Europe, Japan, and North America. The first is to supply them with exotic tropical fruits that do not grow in their cooler climates. Fruits such as lychees, star fruit, and mangos are increasingly air-freighted across the United States from Hawaii to the mainland. Avoiding air miles doesn't mean that we have to give up eating fresh tropical fruit. For decades, bananas have been shipped to cooler countries from the Caribbean and Central America. The fruit is picked before it is ripe and slowly ripens on the ship. Ships carry much more produce and burn less fuel than aircraft.

Luxury foods

The second reason for air-freighting is to supply fresh fruit and vegetables out of season. When food is out of season in the northern hemisphere, it is brought in from the southern hemisphere. It often has to be sent by air, because it would rot if it came by ship. Fresh apricots, strawberries, and blueberries, for example, are air-freighted to Britain from New Zealand. Some crops are imported even when they are in season. Canadian asparagus is flown to Britain, using nine times the amount of energy needed to transport locally grown asparagus.

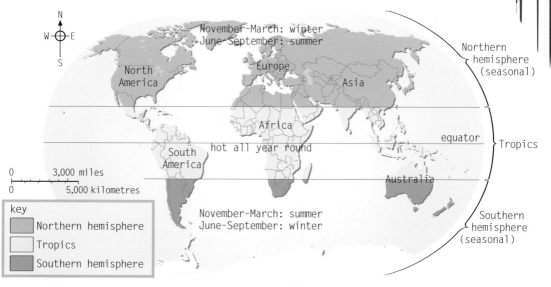

N
W—⊕—E
S

November–March: winter
June–September: summer

North America

Europe

Asia

Africa

hot all year round

South America

equator

Australia

Northern hemisphere (seasonal)

Tropics

Southern hemisphere (seasonal)

0   3,000 miles
0   5,000 kilometres

key
Northern hemisphere
Tropics
Southern hemisphere

November–March: summer
June–September: winter

When it is winter in the northern hemisphere, it is summer in the southern hemisphere. So strawberries ripen in the north in June and in the south in December.

When you buy food direct from a farm, you know that it is fresh and in season.

Shopping solutions

Is there anything you can do to combat the excessive distances that many goods travel before they reach the shops? One thing you can do is to ask where fruit and vegetables come from, and try to choose things grown closest to you. You can also find out what foods are in season and which are produced locally.

Consumer choice

Fruit, vegetables, shellfish, and flowers are flown across the world to provide us with more choice, so the most effective thing to do is to not buy them. Supermarkets in particular pay a lot of attention to what customers say, and what they do and don't buy. If the label on an item of food does not tell you which country it comes from, then ask one of the shop assistants. Write to the company and tell them if you think they should not sell air-freighted goods.

What's in season?

Food companies put a lot of effort into how food looks, but it is how it tastes that really matters. Fresh food tastes better and locally grown food should be the freshest. If you are not sure what foods are in season, ask someone who grows food in their own garden. Most fruit ripens in the summer and early autumn. Salad vegetables usually grow best in summer, but there are many vegetables that are in season in winter, including root vegetables and green vegetables such as winter kale.

Supermarkets now pay such low prices to farmers that more and more farmers are selling their produce direct to shoppers at farmers' markets. Local markets and farm shops are the best way of buying fresh, local food that is in season. Instead of having no link with the way the food was produced, you often buy it from the farmers themselves!

No choice

With many goods it is impossible to know how far the materials and ingredients have travelled before they get to you, and some goods are not available except as cheap imports. The outer layer of a football, for example, consists of several pieces sewn together by hand. It takes three hours and is often done by children in southern Asia. If a worker in Europe or North America were paid to do this work the ball would be many times more expensive.

One way to cut down on food miles is to grow some of your own food, such as this pot of basil.

This warehouse stocks more books than any bookshop. It supplies people who order through the Internet.

FUTURISTIC OR FANTASTICAL?

RepRap is an extraordinary invention developed by scientists at Bath University in Britain. The machine is like a three-dimensional printer. Instead of squirting ink from a nozzle it squirts plastic to build copies of 3D shapes, such as toys. The inventors claim that RepRap will eventually be able to make almost everything. The instructions for the shapes would be bought or shared on the Internet. This would cut out the need not only for shops, but for many factories too, and so cut even more carbon **emissions**.

The end of shops?

The example of the amount of carbon dioxide created in the production and distribution of a CD (see page 12) showed that most was produced by transporting the CD to shops. But this did not include all the tonnes of carbon dioxide produced by the people who travelled to and from the shop to buy the CD. Perhaps the answer is to get rid of shops. Sounds crazy? Maybe, but it is already beginning to happen.

Shopping from home

People already use alternative ways of shopping. You can buy almost everything through the Internet or from catalogues. All the main stores have websites where you can browse and buy what you want. Buying from catalogues and websites gives you the same guarantees that you would get from buying in a shop and the goods are delivered direct to your door. Television shopping channels also offer goods for sale.

Shopping from home certainly saves petrol, or does it? One problem is that people are often not in when their parcels are delivered and so they have to travel to the sorting office to collect them. Another problem is that small, independent shops lose the local customers they rely on. Shopping from shops you can walk to uses the least energy.

Superstores or warehouses?

British ecologist George Monbiot has suggested that superstores should become warehouses. Instead of thousands of people driving to a shopping mall, they would order what they wanted on the Internet and the goods would be delivered to them. Converting superstores to warehouses would save more than petrol. Shops use huge amounts of energy in lighting, heating, and cooling. Supermarkets, for example, display many foods in open cool cabinets. The cabinets keep the food fresh, but they cool the air in the store too, which means that the heating has to be turned up even higher!

Goods ordered by Internet are delivered to your door.

Sustainable farming?

As the population of the world increases, farmers need to produce more and more food. Today's crops produce higher **yields** (more food per plant) than ever before and the same is true of non-food crops, such as rubber and palm oil. The way most crops are grown, however, is producing millions of tonnes of extra carbon dioxide and damaging large areas of the planet. For these reasons, environmentalists say that modern farming methods are unsustainable.

This land used to be rainforest. Now the soil is thin and it will soon be unable to support plants.

Increasing yields

For the last 300 years farmers have been selectively breeding farm crops and animals to get better yields. They have, for example, bred fatter sheep and apples that are larger and sweeter. Today, however, scientists have the ability to put **genes** from one living thing into another to produce a plant or animal that could never occur naturally.

In the past, farmers used the manure of farm animals to nourish the soil the plants grew in. Now most farmers use chemical **fertilizers** to feed their plants and they spray them with chemical **pesticides** to destroy weeds and pests. All of these chemicals use energy for their manufacture and some produce dangerous greenhouse gases.

Destruction of forests

At one time most of Europe was covered with forests that were gradually cut down to make farmland. Today huge machines are felling trees in rainforests in South and Central America to clear the land to farm cows for beef. Cows reared on this land have less fat than other animals and so are much prized by companies that sell beefburgers in North America and other countries.

Large areas of rainforests in South-East Asia are burned by companies that clear the land to grow palm oil, rubber, and other products that they sell to developed countries. Living trees soak up carbon dioxide but, when they are burned, they produce carbon dioxide. Burning forests now accounts for up to a fifth of the world's excess carbon dioxide. Apart from destroying the habitats of millions of species, it creates huge clouds of smoke that choke towns and cities across the whole region.

Huge plantations of oil palms are grown to make biofuels - fuels for transport made from plants instead of from oil and other products.

SOURCE OF NEW PRODUCTS

Rainforests contain more species than any other habitat and new species are being discovered all the time. Chickens, corn, and many common food crops and animals originated in the rainforest. Scientists think that cures for cancers and other diseases could be discovered here too. The Earth cannot afford to lose the rainforests!

Fertilizers allow farmers to get better yields but they add to global warming and can damage the environment.

Chemicals and factory farming

Today most modern farms are run like factories. Chemical fertilizers allow farmers to grow the same crop on the same land, year after year. Growing just one crop is called **monoculture** and it encourages pests that like to feed on it. Farmers kill the pests by spraying the crops with chemical pesticides. Producing chemicals consumes large amounts of energy. Animals are often reared indoors and fed on artificial feeds. This kind of farming, called **factory farming**, allows farmers to produce more food more cheaply, but it is one of the biggest contributors to global warming.

Farming with chemicals

Chemical fertilizers make plants grow even when the natural nutrients in the soil are exhausted. Chemical fertilizers, however, produce nitrous oxide, a greenhouse gas that traps 300 times more heat than the same weight of carbon dioxide. It takes much less nitrous oxide than carbon dioxide to increase global warming.

Insects, field mice, and other small animals feed on the same crops as we do. Farmers poison them with chemicals called pesticides. Diseases such as potato blight flourish in large areas of one crop. Farmers protect their crops by spraying them with more chemicals. Cotton is sprayed with more pesticides than any other crop.

Cotton-workers and people who live near cotton fields frequently suffer from pesticide poisoning. Apples are prone to several diseases and are sprayed up to seven times, as they ripen on the trees. Some of the chemicals remain in the foods we eat and may damage our health.

Farm animals

Chickens and other farm animals do not escape chemicals. Instead of living outside, large factory farms keep huge amounts of animals indoors. Because the animals are crowded together, diseases easily take hold and spread. Farmers combat diseases by injecting the animals with **antibiotics** before they are even ill. Dairy cattle are also given large doses of **hormones** to make them produce more milk. We take in some of these antibiotics and hormones when we eat or drink the food.

Growing cotton is sprayed up to 20 times with pesticides that damage the workers' health too.

GROWN OR MINED?
So much fossil fuel is used by the food industry that many ecologists now claim that our food is "mined", rather than grown. Farming is responsible for about a quarter of the carbon dioxide emitted by the food industry. Farmers burn petrol and diesel oil in tractors, sprayers, combine harvesters, and other farm machinery, while weed-killers, fertilizers, and pesticides are manufactured from oil using fossil fuels.

25

Many people, in Europe and the United States, are opposed to genetically modified food. These people are protesting.

Genetically modified

For hundreds of years farmers have bred plants and animals to increase their yields. By carefully selecting, for example, which bulls to breed with which cows, they have produced cows that give more milk. This is called **selective breeding** because it selects particular characteristics. **Genetic modification**, however, introduces characteristics from one species into another. Ecologists say that genetic modification is not only unnatural, it is dangerous.

How does genetic modification work?

Breeding occurs when genes from a female unite with genes from a male to form a new and different individual. In nature females can only breed with males of the same species. Scientists now, however, are able to add genes from one species to the genes of another species. They might, for example, introduce a gene from a different plant into tomato genes to make tomato plants that are resistant to a particular disease.

Problems with GM

The main argument against GM is that we do not know what the long-term effects of tampering with nature will be. For example, one company genetically modifies seeds so that they are resistant to a powerful **herbicide** that kills weeds. Some of these weeds, however, belong to the same species as the crop. This means that they can breed with the GM plants, producing superweeds that are also resistant to herbicides.

People are also concerned about the long-term effects on humans. With GM, it is impossible to know exactly what you are eating. Someone who has an allergy to nuts, for example, could eat wheat that includes genes from nuts and become ill.

Who will benefit?

GM companies claim that their products will save the world from famine, but most genetic modifications are aimed at consumers in developed countries, not at providing food for the poor. The seeds are expensive and many GM seeds have to be used with a particular pesticide, which is an additional cost.

TERMINATOR SEEDS

Terminator seeds are one idea GM companies have for making money. Usually farmers save some seeds from their harvest to plant the following year, but terminator seeds do not produce fertile seeds. Instead farmers would be forced to buy new seeds from the GM company every year – an extra cost for poor farmers. Ecologists say this is immoral. In 2007 the **United Nations** banned terminator seeds for the time being, but will the ban last?

Genetically modified crops are common in the United States. Food is produced from a mixture of non-GM crops and GM crops, so consumers do not know which they are eating.

Free-range hens can go outside and have more space than factory-farmed hens.

Organic farming

Organic farming is really traditional farming. It uses farming methods developed over centuries to keep the soil and plants healthy. Organic farming avoids chemical fertilizers and pesticides and uses about a quarter of the energy that modern farms use.

Traditional methods

In the past, each farmer grew several different crops. They rotated them so that each field grew a different crop from the previous year. In this way pests and diseases that target a particular crop did not become established. Every year one field would not be planted and this gave the soil a chance to recover its nutrients. Organic farmers use this system of **crop rotation**. Instead of using chemical fertilizers that create huge amounts of nitrous oxide (see page 24), organic farmers use natural fertilizers, such as animal manure, and every three years they plant peas and other crops that fix nitrogen in the ground instead of releasing it into the air. Since plants grown organically are less prone to disease, they do not have to be sprayed as **intensively produced crops** do.

Organic farms and farms that produce **free-range** meat allow their animals to go outside and live more natural lives, as they used to in the past. Free-range animals are healthier than factory-farmed animals and are not routinely given antibiotics.

Advantages

Free-range and organically farmed animals are treated more humanely than factory-farmed animals. Because the animals are free to move around and are fed a natural diet, many people think that the meat tastes better too. Organic crops are free of poisonous sprays and so are healthier for us. More farm workers are needed on organic farms, so it provides more jobs. This is particularly useful in developing countries.

Disadvantages

Plants grown organically do not produce as big a crop as plants grown using modern farming methods, and fruit often has more blemishes. Blemishes, however, only affect the way that something looks, not the way it tastes. More and more people are buying organic food – so many people, in fact, that local farms cannot supply enough. Instead supermarkets buy much of their organic produce from abroad, so adding to global warming by increasing freight miles.

CAN WE AFFORD CHEAP FOOD?

Organic food is often more expensive than non-organic food. Food produced using modern farming methods is cheap but it damages the environment and produces tonnes of extra greenhouse gases. We do not pay for this damage in the price of the food, but we shall pay for global warming in the future. Is the cost of cheap food worth it?

Although organic fruit and vegetables do not contain pesticides and other chemicals, you still have to wash them before you eat them.

Waste mountain

Consumer goods are so cheap that people buy more and more, and many are wasted. Most people replace their mobile phone handsets every 18 months or so, throwing away the old one. Similarly computers are quickly replaced – more than 20 million are thrown away each year in the United States. Many people buy clothes and shoes that they scarcely wear. If a cheap garment stretches after a few washes, they throw it away. Added to this waste is all the packaging that surrounds new items, resulting in a mountain of rubbish.

Packaging

Goods are packaged to keep them clean and to protect them from being damaged in transit. Packaging is also designed to make the goods look more attractive and enticing. Computer games, for example, which consist of a CD-ROM are sold in boxes which are much bigger and bulkier than the game. DVDs are often given away free by newspapers. This is a waste in itself, because most people just throw the DVD away. Nevertheless free DVDs are usually packaged in a simple cardboard sleeve, whereas DVDs that you buy come in larger plastic boxes, moulded inside to fit the DVD. To help combat global warming, manufacturers should use minimum packaging, made if possible from recycled materials.

The packaging that surrounds a DVD is very bulky and may create more carbon dioxide to manufacture than the DVD itself.

Adding to global warming

Packaging is often made from plastics, which are made from oil, a fossil fuel. Plastic is light and can be manufactured into many flexible materials, including cellophane, polythene, and polystyrene. Whatever the material, however, packaging is made by machines that use electricity generated by burning fossil fuels. So packaging may contribute more to global warming that the actual item you are buying. Once you have unwrapped your new purchase, the packaging is no longer needed and you throw it away.

These shoppers are carrying plastic bags from several different stores. Instead of accepting free plastic bags that will be thrown away, put all your shopping in one reusable bag.

BOTTLED WATER

Drinking water is very healthy, but buying water in plastic bottles, which are thrown away when they are empty, damages the environment and contributes to global warming. In Britain alone more than 5,000 million plastic water bottles are thrown away each year. Plastic does not rot, so most of these bottles are filling up rubbish sites. Instead of buying bottled water, it is better to buy a water filter so that you can filter your tap water instead.

Landfill sites are ugly, attract pests, and produce the greenhouse gas methane.

Disposing of waste

Waste that is not recycled (see pages 38 and 39) has to be disposed of somewhere. Most of it is flattened and buried in the ground. This is called **landfill.** Some of it is burned in **incinerators**, but they produce carbon dioxide and often poisonous fumes. Many countries have rules governing how waste can be disposed of. For example, some products, such as house paint and refrigerators, contain damaging chemicals that have to be disposed of safely. Waste is mainly a problem for the developed countries because these are the countries that buy most consumer goods.

Landfill

Until recently, most rubbish was dumped into large holes in the ground and covered with soil. Today, however, many countries are running out of places to do this. Also landfill itself causes several problems. The rubbish smells, which is unpleasant for people who live nearby, and attracts rats and other pests. The dump also creates continual heavy traffic as rubbish trucks go to and from it.

Some of the rubbish rots, creating methane, a damaging greenhouse gas. At some landfill sites, the methane is collected to use as a less-polluting fuel than oil. At other sites, air and liquid are added to landfill to make it decompose quicker. Non-recyclable plastics, however, do not rot and will remain in the landfill site for hundreds of years.

Incinerators

Incinerators are huge furnaces that burn rubbish. The incinerators are very hot and need to be supplied continually with rubbish. It takes a lot of energy to heat an incinerator to the high temperature it needs, and so, in some places, rubbish that should be recycled is being diverted to incinerators, just to keep the furnaces going. Although some incinerators generate electricity, it is still more wasteful to burn rubbish than to recycle it. Burning rubbish can produce poisonous fumes that are released into the atmosphere. Many people claim that incinerators are unhealthy for people who live nearby. Like landfill sites, they generate heavy traffic from rubbish trucks.

Industrial waste

Industries create huge quantities of waste – 300 million scrap tyres, for example, and around 7.5 billion tonnes (8.3 billion tons) of general industrial waste is produced in the United States each year. Like domestic waste, general industrial waste is disposed of in landfill sites or incinerators.

CUT DOWN ON WASTE

Here are a few ways to reduce waste:

- Buy fewer goods.
- Don't accept plastic bags from shops – only use reusable bags.
- Where possible, choose goods that are lightly packaged.
- Reuse packaging, such as yoghurt pots, wherever possible.

These cosmetics are sold with very little packaging.

33

Act now!

Our desire for consumer goods is fuelling global warming, using up the Earth's resources, and creating vast amounts of rubbish. Manufacturers can change the way they package and distribute goods. Farmers can return to more traditional farming methods, stop using so many chemicals on their crops, and treat their animals more humanely. But we can't wait for manufacturers and farmers to change – we have to act ourselves. Why? Because global warming is happening much faster than scientists previously predicted.

Glaciers are melting faster than scientists predicted.

Running out of time

Scientists used to think that we had several decades before the worst effects of global warming would occur. Although the average temperature of the Earth has increased by less than 1 °Celsius (1.8 °Fahrenheit), glaciers in the Arctic, Antarctic, and on high mountain tops are melting faster than expected. In only a few years, glaciers in Norway have retreated several hundred metres. As these glaciers melt, the water runs out the bottom and eventually into the sea. Where glaciers meet the sea, for example, in Greenland, huge chunks of ice are breaking off (called **calving**) and tipping into the sea, raising sea levels.

Unless we can slow down and halt global warming, large areas of farmland could turn into desert like this.

Trouble ahead

The Earth absorbs about half of the billions of extra tonnes of carbon dioxide we produce each year, but the other half is building up in the atmosphere. Even if we stopped burning all fossil fuels now, the temperature of the Earth will still rise due to the extra carbon dioxide already in the air. We have to act now to stop the Earth warming more than 2 °Celsius (3.6 °Fahrenheit) altogether. If we don't, global warming could spiral out of control.

The rainforests could become so dry that they start to catch alight and eventually burn down completely. The land around the Arctic Ocean is **tundra**, a frozen swamp of partly decayed plants. As the climate warms, the tundra will begin to melt, releasing billions of tonnes of methane and carbon dioxide from the rotting plants. These extra gases will increase global warming still further.

Changing the way we live

The good news is that it is not too late to prevent the worst disasters that global warming will bring if things continue as they are now. Manufacturers and farmers produce masses of cheap goods and cheap food because we buy them, and the more enticing the packaging the more we buy. Choosing carefully what we buy and don't buy will change the way manufacturers and farmers produce goods and sell them to us. Cutting out waste is amazingly effective – it can save up to 30 percent of carbon emissions.

Second-hand clothes can be good value for money. If you like retro clothes, shops like this are a good place to look.

Buy less

Reduce, repair, reuse, and recycle – these are the four ways to reduce consumerism. Most people in developed countries have many more clothes and other things than they need, or can really use. Before you buy something, stop and think about whether you really need it or are just buying it to make yourself feel good. How many T-shirts or shoes do you actually need? When you do buy something, do not necessarily buy the cheapest option – cheap things often don't last long. Look instead for things that are well made from materials that can be recycled, and by people who were paid fair wages.

Repair

When something breaks down, see if you can get it repaired. It is cheaper to repair shoes, for example, than to buy new ones. Electrical goods can often be repaired. If the item was so cheap it is not worth repairing, think about buying a better quality one next time.

Reuse

Many items can be reused when you have finished with them, particularly clothes, shoes, CDs, books, DVDs, and CD-ROMs. Provided your clothes are in good condition, you can take them to a charity shop. Someone else can get more wear out of them and the money raised will help people in need. Charity shops and second-hand clothes shops are good places to look for clothes to buy. You can often find good quality clothes being sold for cheap prices. You can also buy and sell second-hand goods on auction websites such as eBay.

Eat less meat

You do not have to be totally vegetarian to eat less meat. Too much red meat can be unhealthy, and beef cows take up valuable land that could be used to grow food crops. They also produce huge amounts of methane, a gas that is produced by their digestive systems. Nearly a fifth of all the methane in the air is produced by farm animals! (Methane traps twenty times as much heat as the same weight of carbon dioxide.)

SHOPPING CHECKLIST

- Only buy new things you really need.
- Only buy things that will last – don't buy things that soon break down or wear out.
- Look for clothes made from organic cotton.
- When something breaks down, see if it can be repaired.
- Reuse gift wrapping, envelopes, and everything else you can.
- Look for energy efficiency labels.
- Look to see where the item was made. Use the Internet to find out which companies have a good employment record and which have a bad record.

Vegetarian food is usually healthy and better for the environment.

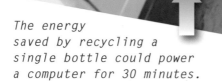

The energy saved by recycling a single bottle could power a computer for 30 minutes.

Recycle

If you can't repair or reuse things you no longer want, then recycle them if possible. Things made of paper, glass, metal, and plastic can all be recycled. This means that the material they are made of is used again and so saves the Earth's resources. It also keeps them out of landfill sites. Manufacturing goods from recycled materials does take energy, but not as much as making them from scratch.

Recycling centres

Many councils collect items to be recycled from your home or you can sort them into special bins for different materials, for example, paper, cardboard, glass of different colours, metals, and plastics. Electronic goods should be recycled to reclaim the parts of them that can be reused.

RECYCLING PAPER

Each tonne of paper that is recycled can save:

- 17 trees
- 1,400 litres of oil
- 26,000 litres of water
- 2 cubic metres of landfill.

To make recycling more efficient, you should wash out bottles and tins first and do not mix in unwanted things, such as plastic wrappers, with the newspapers. Not all plastic things can be recycled – check whether it has a recycling symbol.

Saving resources

Recycling saves raw materials and some energy. Paper is mixed with water to make pulp, instead of cutting down trees to pulp their wood. Whereas new glass is made by heating quartz or silica to a very high temperature, old glass can be melted down at much lower temperatures. It takes 20 times more energy to make a new aluminium can than to recycle a used one. Food scraps and peelings are made into compost, which is full of nutrients and avoids using chemical fertilizers.

BUY RECYCLED GOODS
As well as recycling unwanted things, look for things that are made of recycled materials when you buy something new. Cards and wrapping paper, for example, are often printed on recycled paper.

Making recycling carbon-free

Although recycling saves resources, it does use energy. This is why it is better to reuse and repair rather than recycle. Recycling adds to global warming if it uses electricity that has been generated at a power station that burns fossil fuels. Electricity that has been generated by wind turbines or **solar power** creates much less carbon dioxide.

These glass beads are made of recycled glass.

Look beyond the label

Companies that sell designer labels want you to believe that when you buy their clothes you are buying into a whole way of life. They want you to feel cool, up-to-the-minute and someone to be respected, but, of course, all you are actually buying is a pair of trainers or an item of clothing. Designer labels are expensive because so much money is spent on advertising them. If you look beyond the label, you will often find that the way the company's goods are produced is often not cool or fair. Their factories are usually in developing countries. The workers have to labour long hours in unhealthy conditions, and are paid wages so low they can scarcely feed their families. There is an alternative – it is called **fair trade**.

Fair trade

Fair trade is a system that ensures that the people who produce a crop or work in a factory are paid a fair amount. The extra they are paid makes a big difference to them, but only adds a small amount to the price we pay. Many fair trade agreements are for food crops, such as chocolate, coffee, and bananas. The workers who benefit from them often work together in village **co-operatives.** This means that they share the work and the money they receive equally. They often use some of the profits to benefit the whole village by investing in clean water, schools, and medical care.

These are the logos to look for! You will see them on fair trade products – that is on products where the people who produce them have been fairly paid.

Problems with fair trade

Many people do not want to buy goods that exploit people in developing countries and are keen to buy fair trade goods instead. Even large companies are beginning to offer fair trade goods, which is good news, but be careful. Some companies label their products fair trade when only part of the process qualifies for the label. For example, a garment may be labelled fair trade because the cotton was produced under a fair trade agreement, although the garment itself was made in a **sweatshop** in Bangladesh.

Many café chains include a fair trade option on their menu, but should all the options be fair trade?

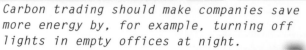

Carbon trading should make companies save more energy by, for example, turning off lights in empty offices at night.

The bigger picture

You can influence companies by what you do and don't buy, and you can help to slow down global warming by buying fewer new things and by reusing, repairing, and recycling old things. But you need to think wider than that. Try to persuade your friends to change the way they shop and dispose of rubbish too. Does your school recycle rubbish, for example? Does it waste resources? Schools use far more energy than a single family, and big companies with many offices use more energy still.

Carbon trading

In 2006 the world's people were producing around 70 billion tonnes (77 billion tons) of carbon dioxide – twice as much as the Earth can absorb. If countries agreed, they could calculate how much carbon dioxide each could safely emit to cut the total by half. Then within a country each large company and institution, such as hospitals, schools, and government offices, could be allowed to emit a safe amount of carbon dioxide. This is part of the idea behind **carbon trading**.

In carbon trading, large companies are each allocated a certain amount of carbon dioxide. If a company exceeds its permitted amount, it can buy extra allowances from companies that have emitted less. In this way "clean" companies make money. Some European countries are trying this idea, but it will only work if the permitted amounts are set low enough. The danger is that the biggest and most polluting companies will simply carry on as they are instead of reducing their pollution.

China and India

The countries that create most greenhouse gases per head are the developed industrialized countries in Europe, North America, and Australasia. These countries need to reduce their carbon dioxide emissions by more than half, because developing countries will emit more as they become industrialized too. China and India are industrializing fast and their carbon dioxide emissions are increasing. If countries agree to set limits, they need to take into account that much of the carbon dioxide developing countries emit is from factories and farms that are producing goods and crops for the developed countries.

Toys made from soft-drink cans. People in developing countries are adept at reusing materials to make new objects.

Glossary

air-freight transport goods by aeroplane

antibiotics medicines that kill bacteria

calving way a glacier produces icebergs as the end of the glacier breaks off and falls into the sea

carbon dioxide gas that is found mainly in the atmosphere

carbon trading system whereby companies and/or countries are each allocated a weight of carbon (that is carbon dioxide) they can produce. Companies or countries that produce more than their allocation buy extra allowances from companies or countries that produce less than their allocation.

chlorofluorocarbons Chlorofluorocarbons (also known as CFCs) are used in refrigerators and other products. When they are released into the air they become greenhouse gases and damage the ozone layer.

climate change change in the usual patterns of climate

co-operatives organization whose members own the business

crop rotation system of farming in which different crops are grown in each field each year

developed country nation, such as the United States or Australia, with a high standard of living due to its advanced economy

developing country nation, such as Kenya or India, where most people rely on farming and are poorer than those in developed nations

drought unusual shortage of rain

emission release of waste substances into the environment, particularly into the atmosphere, rivers, or the sea

factory farming system of farming that mass-produces animals and crops, usually using chemicals and other intensive methods of farming

fair trade trade that is overseen by organizations to make sure that it is fair. This means that goods are bought from producers at a fair price – one that provides an income on which workers can survive.

fertilizers substances that give plants the nutrients they need to grow well

fossil fuels coal, oil, and natural gas. These fuels are called fossil fuels because they formed millions of years ago.

free-range system of farming animals in which the animals are given space to move around

genes parts of living cells that are passed from parents to offspring and determine the biological make-up of the offspring

genetic modification scientific process in which the genes from one species are introduced into a different species

global warming increase in the average temperature of the surface of the Earth

greenhouse gas gas in the atmosphere that traps the Sun's heat and so leads to global warming

herbicide chemical poison used to kill unwanted plants

hormones chemicals produced by a plant or animal that helps to control how the plant or animal functions

hurricane very severe storm involving strong winds over 118 kph (74 mph) and heavy rain

incinerator furnace for burning things such as waste

intensively produced crops crops that are grown year after year on the same land with the help of fertilizers and other chemicals

landfill way of disposing of rubbish by burying it in deep holes in the ground

methane natural gas and one of the greenhouse gases

minimum wage lowest rate of pay that it is legal to pay in a particular country

monoculture system of farming in which only one crop is grown year after year

nitrous oxide one of the greenhouse gases, mostly produced through farming

organic farming method of farming that uses antiobiotics only when necessary and minimal or no artificial fertilizers or other chemicals

pesticides poisons that kill pests, particularly those that attack crops

photosynthesis process in which carbon dioxide from the air and water is combined using chlorophyll and the energy of sunlight to produce sugar. Photosynthesis produces oxygen as a waste gas.

power station building or complex of devices that generates large amounts of electricity

rainforest forest that grows in warm, wet areas of the world. Most rainforest grows in the tropics and contains millions of different species of plants and animals.

refinery building in which oil is refined, or separated, into different substances

regulated controlled

selective breeding breeding farm animals to produce preferred characteristics

solar power using the energy of sunlight or the heat of the Sun to generate electricity

sweatshop clothes factory in which the workers are paid very low wages

synthetic materials materials, such as plastic, nylon, and acrylic, that are made from oil

terminator seeds seeds that have been genetically modified so that the plants they grow into do not produce fertile seeds that can be used to grow more plants the following year

tundra treeless area of land that borders the Arctic and is also found just below the permanent snows of high mountains

turbine device that rotates to generate electricity

typhoon name given to a hurricane in South-East Asia

United Nations (UN) international organization to which most countries belong. The United Nations aims to promote co-operation between nations to encourage economic development and maintain peace.

yields output that is harvested

Further information

Some websites, such as www.hydrogen.co.uk, give information about specific topics – in this case, the potential and benefits of using hydrogen as a fuel. Other websites give information about many aspects of global warming, its consequences, and what you can do. This is a selection of both kinds of websites:

Global warming

www.bbc.co.uk/climate/
Website produced by the BBC. It explains simply and clearly the greenhouse effect, the impact of global warming, and the adaptations we shall need to make. Go to Adaptation and then Life at Home to see what you can do.

www.epa.gov/climatechange/
Website of the US Environmental Protection Agency, which explains global warming and its effect on the environment and ecosystems and suggests various things you can do.

www.ecocentre.org.uk/global-warming. html
Explains the greenhouse effect and where greenhouse gases come from.

climate.wri.org/topic_data_trends.cfm
Gives a world map in which the area of each country is in proportion to the weight of carbon dioxide it emits.

www.energyquest.ca.gov/story/ chapter08.html
Explains how coal, oil, and natural gas were formed.

www.commondreams.org/ headlines06/0312-03.htm
Gives an article published in the *Observer* newspaper about tipping points in the Arctic and how they will accelerate global warming.

www.climatehotmap.org/
A website that gives a map showing early warning signs of global warming in different continents. Produced by several organizations including World Resources Institute, Environmental Defense, and World Wildlife Fund.

*www.earthinstitute.columbia.edu/ crosscutting/climate.htm*l
Website of the Earth Institute at Columbia University in the US. It outlines the consequences of global warming and suggests some things you can do.

www.greenpeace.org.uk/climate/ climatechange/index.cfm
Website of UK environmental campaigning organization, Greenpeace, with facts and predictions concerning global warming.

www.sierraclub.org/globalwarming/qa/
Website covering global warming and things you can do about it.

www.climatecrisis.net/
Website for the film *An Inconvenient Truth*, which includes facts about global warming and things you can do.

green.itweek.co.uk/science/index.html
A website that gives you up-to-date news about developments in green technology.

MAKING THE OCEAN BLOOM

Australian scientist Ian Jones has discovered that adding a fertilizer to the oceans increases the number of phytoplankton – the microscopic plants that feed the oceans' food chains. Like land plants, they absorb carbon dioxide from the air and, when they die, they sink to the bottom of the ocean, taking the carbon dioxide with them. The best fertilizer he has found is urea – one of the ingredients of urine!

Air miles

www.guardian.co.uk/kenya/ story/0,,1928004,00.html
How flower companies are depriving Kenyan farmers of much-needed water.

Cotton

www.stepin.org/casestudy. php?id=ecofashion&page=9
Educational website comparing organic cotton and cotton grown with pesticides. Click on "Eco-fashion" to find out more.

Food and fossil fuel

www.corporatewatch.org.uk/?lid=2713
Tells you about fossil fuel – how the food energy depends on fossil foods.

www.ecoliteracy.org/publications/rsl/tom-starrs.html
Tells you about fossil fuel and how you can choose your food to reduce the amount of carbon dioxide.

Organic farming

www.soilassociation.org/web/sa/saweb. nsf/living/index.html
Website of the Soil Association, an organization that campaigns for organic farming, giving you reasons to buy organic products.

www.newscientist.com/article. ns?id=dn6496
Article from the *New Scientist* magazine about how organic farming helps diversity.

Hydrogen fuel

www.hydrogen.co.uk/h2/hydrogen.htm
Gives diagram showing how hydrogen could be produced from renewable sources of electricity and used to power buildings and transport.

Carbon offsetting

www.carbonfootprint.com/calculator.html
Website that allows you to calculate how much carbon your family produces.

Index

air-freight 14–15, 16, 17, 18, 29
animal welfare 25, 29
antibiotics 25, 28

carbon dioxide 8–9, 11, 16
    absorption 35
    emissions 22, 23, 25, 30, 32, 35, 42
    emissions, reducing 20, 35, 43
carbon "sinks" 11
carbon trading 42–43
CD manufacture 12, 20
cheap food 29, 35
cheap goods 4, 35
child labour 4, 19
chlorofluorocarbons (CFCs) 11
climate change 6–7
clothing industry 40, 41
coal 10
consumer choice 18, 19, 35
cotton 14, 24, 37, 47
crop rotation 28

droughts 6, 7

electricity
    consumption 5, 10
    generating 5, 10, 11, 33, 39

factory farming 24, 25
fair trade 40–41, 47
farm shops 19
farmers' markets 19
farming 14, 15, 22–29, 34
    carbon dioxide emissions 22, 25
    crop yields 22
factory farming 24, 25
fertilizers, herbicides, and pesticides 22, 24, 25, 27, 28, 39
flooding 6, 7
flowers 14, 15
food industry 14, 15, 16–17, 18–19, 25
food miles 16–17, 29

fossil fuels 5, 7, 8, 9, 10, 12, 14, 25, 31, 35, 47
free-range farming 28, 29
    genetically modified food 26–27, 47
    monocultures 24
    non-food crops 22, 23
    organic farming 28, 29, 47

genetically modified (GM) food 26–27, 47
global warming 5, 6, 46
    causes 8, 24
    contribution of consumerism to 5, 12, 13, 16, 24, 34
    effects of 6–7
greenhouse gases 11, 22, 24, 29, 32, 43

hurricanes and typhoons 7

ice, melting 7, 34
incinerators 32, 33
industrial waste 33
industrialized countries 13, 43
Internet shopping 21

landfill sites 32, 38
local and seasonal food 18, 19
low pay 4, 14, 15, 40, 41

manufacturing 12–13
meat eating 37
methane 11, 32, 35, 37
monocultures 24

natural gas 10
nitrous oxide 11, 24, 28

oil 10, 31
    products 11
    refining 10, 11
organic farming 28, 29, 47

packaging 30–31, 34, 35
pesticide poisoning 25

photosynthesis 8
plastics 31, 32, 39
power stations 10, 11
producer–consumer relation 13

rainforests 11, 23, 35
    destruction 23
    products 23
recycling 30, 36, 38–39, 42, 43, 47
repairing goods 36, 37, 39, 42
reusing goods 36, 37, 39, 42, 43

sea levels, rising 7, 34
second-hand good 36
selective breeding 22, 26
shopping bonanza 4
shopping checklist 37
shopping solutions 18–19, 21, 42, 43
solar power 39
synthetic materials 5, 9, 11

terminator seeds 27
transport and
    distribution 10, 14–15, 16, 20, 34
tundra 35
turbines 10, 39

vegetarian food 37

warehouses 21
waste 30–33
    disposal 32–33
    reducing 33, 35
water resources, depletion of 15
water vapour 11

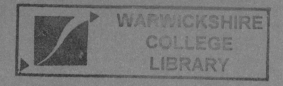